ROYAL COURT

The Royal Court Theatre & Mighty Mouth Ltd present

# NOT I / FOOTFALLS / ROCKABY

by **Samuel Beckett**

This production of NOT I / FOOTFALLS / ROCKABY was first performed at the Royal Court Jerwood Theatre Downstairs, Sloane Square, on Thursday 9th January 2014.

# NOT I / FOOTFALLS / ROCKABY

by **Samuel Beckett**

*Performed by*
**Lisa Dwan**

Director **Walter Asmus**
Designer **Alex Eales**
Lighting Designer **James Farncombe**
Composer **Tom Smail**
Sound Designer **David McSeveney**
Stage Manager **Cath Binks**
Assistant Director **Matthew McFrederick**
Production Manager **Niall Black**
Set Constructed by **Factory Settings**
Produced in association with **Cusack Projects Ltd**

Lisa Dwan first performed NOT I in a production directed by Natalie Abrahami, designed by Michael Vale with lighting design by Katharine Williams.

The Royal Court and Stage Management would like to thank J.D. McDougall for their help with this production.

# THE COMPANY

## SAMUEL BECKETT (Writer)

Samuel Beckett (1906-1989) is widely recognised as one of the greatest dramatists of the twentieth century. He was awarded the Nobel Prize for Literature in 1969.

Beckett is most renowned for his play Waiting for Godot which launched his career in theatre. He then went on to write numerous successful full-length plays, including Endgame in 1957, Krapp's Last Tape in 1958 and Happy Days in 1960. Beckett received his first commission for radio from the BBC in 1956 for All That Fall. This was followed by a further five plays for radio including Embers, Words and Music and Cascando.

Like no other dramatist before him, Beckett's works capture the pathos and ironies of modern life yet still maintain his faith in man's capacity for compassion and survival no matter how absurd his environment may have become.

## WALTER ASMUS (Director)

THEATRE INCLUDES: Uncle Vanya (Staatstheater Darmstadt); Oedipus, Antigone, Maria Magdalena (Staatstheater Karlsruhe); The Oresteia (Glocksee Centre, Hanover); Waiting for Godot (BAM New York; Riverside Studios; Gate, Dublin; Betty Nansen; Teatret Copenhagen; 7Stages, Atlanta; Rubicon, Ventura CA); Endgame (Bristol Music Centre; Teatret, Copenhagen; Theater Freiburg; Stary Teatr, Cracow; Dramatic Arts Center, Shanghai); Krapp's Last Tape (Bristol Teatret Copenhagen; 7Stages, Atlanta); Beckett's Shorter Plays (Berlin/Hamburg/Hanover/Darmstadt/Cracow/Copenhagen/Rubicon, Ventura CA/Atlanta); Adaptation of First Love (Sydney Writers' Festival at Sydney Theatre Company).

TELEVISION INCLUDES: Waiting for Godot, Krapp's Last Tape, Rockaby, Footfalls, What Where.

FILM INCLUDES: Footfalls.

RADIO INCLUDES: Company.

Walter was Artist in Residence at the Metabolic Studio (The Annenberg Foundation), LA, 2010.

## LISA DWAN (Performer)

FOR THE ROYAL COURT: Not I.

OTHER THEATRE INCLUDES: Illusions (Bush); Queen Margot, Diary Of An Unhappy Queen (Barbican); Beside the Sea (Southbank Centre); Not I (Southbank Centre/BAC); A Soldier's Tale (Hay Festival); Whiskey in the Jar (Soho); The Importance of Being Earnest (Irish tour); History of the World at 3am (Andrews Lane); As You Like It (Nun's Island).

TELEVISION INCLUDES: Not I, Rock Rivals, Fair City, The Big Bow Wow, Mystic Knights.

FILM INCLUDES: The Engagement, Walt Disney's Oliver Twist, Tailor of Panama, Bhopal - A Prayer for Rain, Moving Target, Lord Lucan, Sparrowhawk.

## ALEX EALES (Designer)

AS COSTUME DESIGNER, FOR THE ROYAL COURT: Iron (&Traverse/Schauspielhaus, Leipzig).

AS DESIGNER, THEATRE INCLUDES: Alles weitere kennen Sie aus dem Kino (Deutsches Schauspielhaus Hamburg); Fraulein Julie (Schaubühne, Berlin/Barbican); Reise durch die Nacht (Schauspielhaus, Cologne, Berlin & Avignon festival); Brimstone & Treacle, Ghosts (Arcola); Design For Living (Salisbury Playhouse); Say It With Flowers, small hours (Hampstead); The Breath Of Life (Lyceum Theatre, Sheffield); Dyled Eileen, Spring Awakening - the Musical (Theatr Genedlaethol/tour); The Devil Inside Him (National Theatre Wales); Wunschkonzert (Schauspielhaus, Cologne & Berlin); Jungfruleken (Kungsliga Dramatiska Teatern, Stockholm); The Swallowing Dark (Liverpool Playhouse Studio & Theatre 503); The Caucasian Chalk Circle, The Resistible Rise Of Arturo Ui (Watford Palace/Tour); At Break Of Day, Widows, R.U.R , Still Life (Drum Theatre, Plymouth); The Country (Belgrade Theatre at Warwick Arts Centre).

AS DESIGNER, OPERA INCLUDES: The House Taken Over (Festival d'Aix-en-Provence); Cosi fan Tutte (Opera Holland Park); Clemency (ROH2 Linbury Studio/Scottish Opera); Idomeneo (English National Opera); Tarantula in Petrol Blue (Aldeburgh Music); The Crocodile (Arcola).

## JAMES FARNCOMBE (Lighting Designer)

FOR THE ROYAL COURT: Love, Love, Love, The Village Bike.

OTHER THEATRE INCLUDES: Edward II, London Road, Men Should Weep, People, The Magistrate, Double Feature (National); Juno & the Paycock (National/Abbey); The Rest Will Be Familiar to You From Cinema (Deutsche Schauspielhaus, Hamburg); As You Like It, Mad World My Masters (RSC); Three Sisters, The Changeling, The Glass Menagerie (Young Vic); The Duchess of Malfi (Old Vic); The Recruiting Officer, Inadmissible Evidence (Donmar); Jeeves & Wooster 'Perfect Nonsense' (Duke of York's); The Ladykillers (Gielgud/Vaudeville); Ghost Stories (Liverpool Playhouse/Lyric Hammersmith/Duke of York's/Toronto); Swallows & Amazons (Vaudeville); Juliet & Her Romeo, Far Away (Bristol Old Vic); Desire Under the Elms, Twisted Tales (Lyric Hammersmith); Osama the Hero, Taking Care of Baby, Longing, Rapture Blister Burn (Hampstead).

DANCE INCLUDES: Firebird (Norwegian National Ballet, Oslo).

OPERA INCLUDES: La Vin Herbé (Berlin Staatsoper); The House Taken Over (Aix-en-Provence Festival); The Flying Dutchman (Scottish Opera).

## DAVID MCSEVENEY (Sound Designer)

FOR THE ROYAL COURT: The Djinns of Eidgah, Routes, If You Don't Let Us Dream We Won't Let You Sleep, Constellations (& West End), Belong, Vera Vera Vera, The Village Bike, Clybourne Park (& West End), Ingredient X, Posh (& West End), Disconnect, Cock, A Miracle, The Stone, Shades, Seven Jewish Children, The Girlfriend Experience (& Theatre Royal Plymouth/Young Vic), Contractions, Fear & Misery/War & Peace.

OTHER THEATRE INCLUDES: The Changeling, A Doll's House (Young Vic/West End); The Duke in Darkness (Tabard); The Winter's Tale (RSC); Stones in His Pockets (Tricycle); Victoria Station/One for the Road (Print Room/Young Vic); On the Record (Arcola); Tin Horizon (503); Gaslight (Old Vic); Charley's Aunt, An Hour & a Half Late (Theatre Royal Bath); A Passage to India, After Mrs Rochester, Madame Bovary (Shared Experience); Men Should Weep, Rookery Nook (Oxford Stage Company); Othello (Southwark Playhouse).

David is Head of Sound at the Royal Court.

## MATTHEW MCFREDERICK (Assistant Director)

AS DIRECTOR, THEATRE INCLUDES: And of the Son (& Nun's Island), Beckett Shorts: Breath, Rockaby, Catastrophe, Not I, Come & Go (Brian Friel Theatre, Belfast).

AS PERFORMER, THEATRE INCLUDES: Emerald Isle Theatre Company (European Tour).

Matthew is an AHRC PhD student and sessional teacher at the University of Reading.

## TOM SMAIL (Composer)

THEATRE INCLUDES: A Scattering (Robert Bathurst).

TELEVISION INCLUDES: Daphne, Daniel Libeskind, The New Face of Leprosy, Amazon - Super River, Deadly Vipers, Penguins – Cool Bird in a Hot Spot, Birds Behaving Badly, Mervyn, The Whale That Swam to London, The Riddle of Einstein's Brain, Women at War, Blenheim, The Mysterious Hanging Coffins of China.

FILM INCLUDES: The Verge, The Barn, A Car Stopped, Save the Tiger, Shrink, Ghost Rig.

RADIO INCLUDES: Voices From Another Room, And It Came To Pass, The Moving & The Still, Elephants Can Remember, Dumb Witness, The Mysterious Affair at Styles, The Adventure of the Christmas Pudding, One, Two, Buckle My Shoe.

RECENT CONCERT PERFORMANCES INCLUDE: Music in the Marble (City of London Sinfonia); Soliloquy for Strings (Arch Sinfonia); Jack & the Beanstalk, Red Riding Hood (English Touring Opera); Soon (Tête-à-Tête Opera Festival); String Quartet No.1 (Allegri Quartet); Somewhere Else (Cerne Abbas Festival); The Heart-in-Waiting, In the Bleak Midwinter, Sheep like Stones (St. George's, Hanover Square); What Is the Word, Instructions To Four Walls, Care-charmer Sleep, As Shade to Shadow, Quo Vadis? (Kapoor Chamber Concerts).

# THE ENGLISH STAGE COMPANY AT THE ROYAL COURT THEATRE

*'For me the theatre is really a religion or way of life. You must decide what you feel the world is about and what you want to say about it, so that everything in the theatre you work in is saying the same thing ... A theatre must have a recognisable attitude. It will have one, whether you like it or not.'*

photo: Stephen Cummiskey

George Devine, first artistic director of the English Stage Company: notes for an unwritten book.

As Britain's leading national company dedicated to new work, the Royal Court Theatre produces new plays of the highest quality, working with writers from all backgrounds, and addressing the problems and possibilities of our time.

"The Royal Court has been at the centre of British cultural life for the past 50 years, an engine room for new writing and constantly transforming the theatrical culture." Stephen Daldry

Since its foundation in 1956, the Royal Court has presented premieres by almost every leading contemporary British playwright, from John Osborne's Look Back in Anger to Caryl Churchill's A Number and Tom Stoppard's Rock 'n' Roll. Just some of the other writers to have chosen the Royal Court to premiere their work include Edward Albee, John Arden, Richard Bean, Samuel Beckett, Edward Bond, Leo Butler, Jez Butterworth, Martin Crimp, Ariel Dorfman, Stella Feehily, Christopher Hampton, David Hare, Eugène Ionesco, Ann Jellicoe, Terry Johnson, Sarah Kane, David Mamet, Martin McDonagh, Conor McPherson, Joe Penhall, Lucy Prebble, Mark Ravenhill, Simon Stephens, Wole Soyinka, Polly Stenham, David Storey, Debbie Tucker Green, Arnold Wesker and Roy Williams.

"It is risky to miss a production there." Financial Times

In addition to its full-scale productions, the Royal Court also facilitates international work at a grass-roots level, developing exchanges which bring young writers to Britain and sending British writers, actors and directors to work with artists around the world. The research and play development arm of the Royal Court Theatre, The Studio, finds the most exciting and diverse range of new voices in the UK. The Studio runs play-writing groups including the Young Writers Programme, Critical Mass for Black, Asian and minority ethnic writers and the biennial Young Writers Festival. For further information, go to www.royalcourttheatre.com/playwriting/the-studio.

Supported by
ARTS COUNCIL
ENGLAND

# ROYAL COURT SUPPORTERS

The Royal Court has significant and longstanding relationships with many organisations and individuals who provide vital support. It is this support that makes possible its unique playwriting and audience development programmes.

Coutts supports Innovation at the Royal Court. The Genesis Foundation supports the Royal Court's work with International Playwrights. Theatre Local is sponsored by Bloomberg. Alix Partners support The Big Idea at the Royal Court. The Jerwood Charitable Foundation supports emerging writers through the Jerwood New Playwrights series. The Andrew Lloyd Webber Foundation supports the Royal Court's Studio,which aims to seek out, nurture and support emerging playwrights. The Harold Pinter Playwright's Award is given annually by his widow, Lady Antonia Fraser, to support a new commission at the Royal Court.

**PUBLIC FUNDING**
Arts Council England, London
British Council
European Commission Representation in the UK

**CHARITABLE DONATIONS**
Martin Bowley Charitable Trust
Columbia Foundation Fund of the London Community Foundation
Cowley Charitable Trust
The Dorset Foundation
The John Ellerman Foundation
The Eranda Foundation
Genesis Foundation
The Golden Bottle Trust
The Haberdashers' Company
The Idlewild Trust
Jerwood Charitable Foundation
Marina Kleinwort Trust
The Andrew Lloyd Webber Foundation
John Lyon's Charity
Clare McIntyre's Bursary
The Andrew W. Mellon Foundation
The David & Elaine Potter Foundation
Rose Foundation
The Royal College of Psychiatrists
Royal Victoria Hall Foundation
The Sackler Trust
The Sobell Foundation
John Thaw Foundation
The Vandervell Foundation
Sir Siegmund Warburg's Voluntary Settlement
The Garfield Weston Foundation

**CORPORATE SUPPORTERS & SPONSORS**
AKA
Alix Partners
American Airlines
BBC
Bloomberg
Café Colbert
Coutts
Fever-Tree
Kudos Film & Television
MAC
Moët & Chandon
Quintessentially Vodka
Smythson of Bond Street
White Light Ltd

**BUSINESS ASSOCIATES, MEMBERS & BENEFACTORS**
Annoushka
Auerbach & Steele Opticians
Bank of America Merrill Lynch
Byfield Consultancy
Capital MSL
Cream
Lazard
Vanity Fair
Waterman Group

**DEVELOPMENT ADVOCATES**
John Ayton MBE
Elizabeth Bandeen
Kinvara Balfour
Anthony Burton CBE
Piers Butler
Sindy Caplan
Sarah Chappatte
Cas Donald (Vice Chair)
Celeste Fenichel
Emma Marsh (Chair)
Deborah Shaw Marquardt (Vice Chair)
Tom Siebens
Sian Westerman
Daniel Winterfeldt

Supported by ARTS COUNCIL ENGLAND

Innovation Partner Coutts

**INDIVIDUAL MEMBERS**

**MAJOR DONORS**
Eric Abraham
Ray Barrell & Ursula Van Almsick
Cas Donald
Lydia & Manfred Gorvy
Richard & Marcia Grand
Jack & Linda Keenan
Adam Kenwright
Miles Morland
Mr & Mrs Sandy Orr
NoraLee & Jon Sedmak
Deborah Shaw & Stephen Marquardt
Jan & Michael Topham
Monica B Voldstad

**MOVER-SHAKERS**
Anonymous
Christine Collins
Jordan Cook
Mr & Mrs Roderick Jack
Duncan Matthews QC
Mr & Mrs Timothy D Proctor
Ian & Carol Sellars

**BOUNDARY-BREAKERS**
Katie Bradford
Piers & Melanie Gibson
David Harding
Madeleine Hodgkin
Philip & Joan Kingsley
Emma Marsh
Edgar & Judith Wallner
Mr & Mrs Nick Wheeler

**GROUNDBREAKERS**
Anonymous
Allen Appen & Jane Wiest
Moira Andreae
Mr & Mrs Simon Andrews
Nick Archdale
Charlotte Asprey
Jane Attias
Elizabeth & Adam Bandeen
Dr Kate Best
Sarah & David Blomfield
Stan & Val Bond
Neil & Sarah Brener
Deborah Brett
Mr & Mrs William Broeksmit
Joanna Buckenham
Lois Moore & Nigel Burridge
Louise Burton
Clive & Helena Butler
Piers Butler
Sindy & Jonathan Caplan
Gavin & Lesley Casey
Sarah & Philippe Chappatte
Tim & Caroline Clark
Carole & Neville Conrad
Andrea & Anthony Coombs
Clyde Cooper
Ian & Caroline Cormack
Mr & Mrs Cross
Andrew & Amanda Cryer
Alison Davies
Roger & Alison De Haan
Matthew Dean
Polly Devlin OBE
Rob & Cherry Dickins
Sophie Diedrichs-Cox
Denise & Randolph Dumas
Robyn Durie
Glenn & Phyllida Earle
The Edwin Fox Foundation
Lisa Erikson & Edward Ocampo
Mark & Sarah Evans
Celeste & Peter Fenichel
Margy Fenwick
Deborah Ferreira
Beverley Gee
Nick & Julie Gould
Lord & Lady Grabiner
Jill Hackel & Andrzej Zarzycki
Carol Hall
Stephen & Jennifer Harper
Mr & Mrs Sam Haubold
Gordon & Brette Holmes
Kate Hudspeth
Damien Hyland
Suzie & David Hyman
Amanda Ibbetson
Melanie J. Johnson
Nicholas Jones
Dr Evi Kaplanis
David P Kaskel & Christopher A Teano
Vincent & Amanda Keaveny
Peter & Maria Kellner
Nicola Kerr
Steve Kingshott
Mr & Mrs Pawel Kisielewski
Mr & Mrs David & Sarah Kowitz
Rosemary Leith
Imelda Liddiard
Daisy & Richard Littler
Kathryn Ludlow
Beatrice & James Lupton CBE
Suzanne Mackie
Dr Ekaterina Malievskaia & George Goldsmith
Christopher Marek Rencki
Mrs Janet Martin
Andrew McIver
Barbara Minto
Takehito Mitsui
Angelie Moledina
Ann & Gavin Neath CBE
Clive & Annie Norton
Georgia Oetker
James Orme-Smith
Mr & Mrs Guy Paterson
Sir William & Lady Vanessa Patey
William Plapinger & Cassie Murray
Andrea & Hilary Ponti
Annie & Preben Prebensen
Wendy & Philip Press
Mrs Ivetta Rabinovich
Julie Ritter
Paul & Gill Robinson
Andrew & Ariana Rodger
Corinne Rooney
William & Hilary Russell
Julie & Bill Ryan
Sally & Anthony Salz
Bhags Sharma
The Michael & Melanie Sherwood Charitable Foundation
Tom Siebens & Mimi Parsons
Andy Simpkin
Anthony Simpson & Susan Boster
Andrea Sinclair & Serge Kremer
Paul & Rita Skinner
Mr & Mrs RAH Smart
Brian Smith
Barbara Soper
Saadi & Zeina Soudavar
Sue St Johns
The Ulrich Family
Amanda Vail
Constanze Von Unruh
Ian & Victoria Watson & The Watson Foundation
Matthew & Sian Westerman
Anne-Marie Williams
Sir Robert & Lady Wilson
Mr Daniel Winterfeldt & Mr Jonathan Leonhart
Martin & Sally Woodcock
Katherine & Michael Yates

With thanks to our Friends, Stage-Taker and Ice-Breaker members whose support we greatly appreciate.

## FOR THE ROYAL COURT

Royal Court Theatre, Sloane Square, London SW1W 8AS
Tel: 020 7565 5050 Fax: 020 7565 5001
info@royalcourttheatre.com, www.royalcourttheatre.com

Artistic Director **Vicky Featherstone**
Associate Directors **Ola Animashawun, Carrie Cracknell, Simon Godwin, John Tiffany**
Trainee Director **Debbie Hannan‡**
Artistic Associate **Emily McLaughlin***
International Director **Elyse Dodgson**
International Associate **Richard Twyman**
Education Associate **Lynne Gagliano***
Education Apprentice **Maia Clarke**
Assistant to the Executive **Kathryn Chin**

Literary Manager **Christopher Campbell**
Deputy Literary Manager **Carissa Hope Lynch***
Assistant Literary Manager **Louise Stephens Alexander**
Trainee Administrator (Literary & Studio) **Hayley Dallimore§**
Writers' Tutor **Leo Butler***

Head of Casting (Maternity Leave) **Amy Ball**
Head of Casting (Maternity Cover) **Julia Horan CDG**
Casting Deputy **Lotte Hines**

Head of Production **Niall Black**
Production Manager **Tariq Rifaat**
Production Assistant **Zoe Hurwitz**
Head of Lighting **Jack Williams**
Deputy Head of Lighting **Marec Joyce**
Lighting Technicians **Jess Faulks, Sam Smallman**
JTD Programmer & Operator **Laura Whitley**
Head of Stage **Steven Stickler**
Stage Deputy **Dan Lockett**
Stage Chargehand **Lee Crimmen**
Chargehand & Building Maintenance Technician **Matt Livesey**
Head of Sound **David McSeveney**
Sound Deputy **Emily Legg**
Sound Operators **Laura Hammond, Chris Payne**
Technical Trainees **Iyce Kariuki, Emily Walker§**

Head of Costume **Iona Kenrick**
Costume Deputy **Jackie Orton**

Executive Producer **Lucy Davies**
General Manager **Catherine Thornborrow**
Administrator **Holly Gladwell**
Projects Manager **Chris James**

Finance Director **Helen Perryer**
Finance Manager **Martin Wheeler**
Finance Officer **Rachel Harrison***
Finance & Administration Assistant **Rosie Mortimer**

Head of Marketing & Sales **Becky Wootton**
Press & Public Relations Officer **Anna Evans**
Marketing Manager (Jobshare) **Ruth Waters & Ruth Hawkins**
Communications Officer **Dion Wilson**
Communications Trainees **Jasdeep Phull, Rachel Pronger§**

Sales Manager **Liam Geoghegan**
Deputy Sales Manager **Áine O'Sullivan**
Box Office Sales Assistants **Ryan Govin*, Joe Hodgson, Chelsea Nelson, Zainab Hassan*, Helen Preddy***

Head of Development **Rebecca Kendall**
Senior Development Manager (Maternity Leave) **Sue Livermore**
Senior Development Manager (Maternity Cover) **Lucy Buxton**
Development Managers **Luciana Lawlor, Anna Sampson**
Development Assistant **Kate Garbutt**

Theatre Manager **Rachel Dudley**
Senior Duty House Manager **Elinor Keber***
Theatre Assistant **Chris Sonnex**
Duty House Managers **Helen Matravers, Mila Rosser***
Bar & Kitchen Manager **Sami Rifaat**
Deputy Bar & Kitchen Manager **Siobhan Lightfoot**
Assistant Bar & Kitchen Manager **Jared Thomas**
Head Chef **Tim Jenner**
Sous Chef **Paulino Chuitcheu**
Bookshop Manager **Simon David**
Bookshop Assistant **Vanessa Hammick***
Stage Door/Reception **Paul Lovegrove, Tyrone Lucas, Jane Wainwright**

Thanks to all of our ushers and bar staff.
§ Posts supported by The Sackler Trust Trainee Scheme
‡ The post of Trainee Director is supported by an anonymous donor.
* Part-time.

### ENGLISH STAGE COMPANY

President
**Dame Joan Plowright CBE**

Honorary Council
**Sir Richard Eyre CBE**
**Alan Grieve CBE**
**Martin Paisner CBE**

Council
Chairman **Anthony Burton CBE**
Vice Chairman **Graham Devlin CBE**

Members
**Jennette Arnold OBE**
**Judy Daish**
**Sir David Green KCMG**
**Joyce Hytner OBE**
**Stephen Jeffreys**
**Wasfi Kani OBE**
**Phyllida Lloyd CBE**
**Emma Marsh**
**James Midgley**
**Sophie Okonedo OBE**
**Alan Rickman**
**Anita Scott**
**Katharine Viner**
**Lord Stewart Wood**

# Not I / Footfalls / Rockaby

Samuel Beckett was born in Dublin in 1906 and graduated from Trinity College. He settled in Paris in 1937, after travels in Germany and periods of residence in London and Dublin. He remained in France during the Second World War and was active in the French Resistance. From the spring of 1946 his plays, novels, short fiction, poetry and criticism were largely written in French. With the production of *En attendant Godot* in Paris in 1953, Beckett's work began to achieve widespread recognition. During his subsequent career as a playwright and novelist in both French and English he redefined the possibilities of prose fiction and writing for the theatre. Samuel Beckett won the Prix Formentor in 1961 and the Nobel Prize in Literature in 1969. He died in Paris in December 1989.

BY SAMUEL BECKETT

*plays*

WAITING FOR GODOT

ALL THAT FALL & OTHER PLAYS FOR RADIO AND SCREEN

ENDGAME

KRAPP'S LAST TAPE & OTHER SHORTER PLAYS

HAPPY DAYS

*prose*

MORE PRICKS THAN KICKS

MURPHY

WATT

MOLLOY

MALONE DIES

THE UNNAMABLE

THE EXPELLED / THE CALMATIVE / THE END / FIRST LOVE

HOW IT IS

TEXTS FOR NOTHING AND OTHER SHORTER PROSE 1950–1976

MERCIER AND CAMIER

COMPANY / ILL SEEN ILL SAID / WORSTWARD HO / STIRRINGS STILL

*poetry*

SELECTED POEMS 1930–1989

SAMUEL BECKETT

# Not I
# Footfalls
# Rockaby

ff

FABER & FABER

This collection first published in 2014
by Faber and Faber Ltd
Bloomsbury House
74–77 Great Russell Street
London WC1B 3DA

Typeset by Country Setting, Kingsdown, Kent
Printed and bound by
CPI Group (UK) Ltd, Croydon, CR0 4YY



A CIP record for this book
is available from the British Library

ISBN 978-0-571-31489-8

2 4 6 8 10 9 7 5 3

# Contents

# Not I

Written in English in spring 1972. First performed at the Forum Theater of the Lincoln Center, New York, in September 1972, directed by Alan Schneider, with Jessica Tandy as Mouth. First published by Faber and Faber, London, in 1973. First performed in Britain at the Royal Court Theatre, London, on 16 January 1973, with Billie Whitelaw as Mouth.

## Note

Movement: this consists in simple sideways raising of arms from sides and their falling back, in a gesture of helpless compassion. It lessens with each recurrence till scarcely perceptible at third. There is just enough pause to contain it as MOUTH recovers from vehement refusal to relinquish third person.

*Stage in darkness but for* MOUTH, *upstage audience right, about eight feet above stage level, faintly lit from close-up and below, rest of face in shadow. Invisible microphone.* AUDITOR, *downstage audience left, tall standing figure, sex undeterminable, enveloped from head to foot in loose black djellaba, with hood, fully faintly lit, standing on invisible podium about four feet high shown by attitude alone to be facing diagonally across stage intent on* MOUTH, *dead still throughout but for four brief movements where indicated. See Note. As house lights down* MOUTH*'s voice unintelligible behind curtain. House lights out. Voice continues unintelligible behind curtain, ten seconds. With rise of curtain ad-libbing from text as required leading when curtain fully up and attention sufficient into:*

MOUTH: . . . out . . . into this world . . . this world . . . tiny little thing . . . before its time . . . in a godfor— . . . what? . . . girl? . . . yes . . . tiny little girl . . . into this . . . out into this . . . before her time . . . godforsaken hole called . . . called . . . no matter . . . parents unknown . . . unheard of . . . he having vanished . . . thin air . . . no sooner buttoned up his breeches . . . she similarly . . . eight months later . . . almost to the tick . . . so no love . . . spared that . . . no love such as normally vented on the . . . speechless infant . . . in the home . . . no . . . nor indeed for that matter any of any kind . . . no love of any kind . . . at any subsequent stage . . . so typical affair . . . nothing of any note till coming up to sixty when — . . . what? . . . seventy? . . . good God! . . . coming up to seventy . . . wandering in a field . . . looking aimlessly for cowslips . . . to make a ball . . . a few steps then stop . . . stare into space . . . then on . . . a few more . . . stop and stare again . . . so on . . . drifting around . . . when suddenly . . . gradually . . . all went out . . . all that early April morning light . . . and she found herself in the — . . . what? . . . who? . . . no! . . . she! . . . [*Pause and movement 1.*] . . . found herself in the dark . . . and if not exactly . . . insentient . . . insentient . . . for she could still hear the buzzing . . . so-called . . . in the ears . . . and a ray of light came and went . . . came and went . . . such as the moon might cast . . . drifting . . . in and out of cloud . . . but so dulled . . . feeling . . . feeling so dulled . . . she did not know . . . what position she was in . . . imagine! . . . what position she was in! . . . whether standing . . . or sitting . . . but the brain — . . . what? . . . kneeling? . . . yes . . . whether standing . . . or sitting . . . or kneeling . . . but the brain — . . . what? . . . lying? . . . yes . . . whether standing . . . or sitting . . . or kneeling . . . or lying . . . but the brain still . . . still . . . in a way . . . for her first thought was . . . oh long after . . . sudden flash . . . brought up as she had been to believe . . . with the other waifs . . . in a merciful . . . [*Brief laugh.*] . . . God . . . [*Good laugh.*] . . . first thought was . . . oh long after . . . sudden flash . . . she was being punished . . . for her sins . . . a number of which then . . . further proof if proof were needed . . . flashed through her mind . . . one after another . . . then dismissed as foolish . . . oh long after . . . this thought dismissed . . . as she suddenly realised . . . gradually realised . . . she was not suffering . . . imagine! . . . not suffering! . . . indeed could not remember . . . off-hand . . . when she had suffered less . . . unless of course she was

. . . *meant* to be suffering . . . ha! . . . *thought* to be suffering . . . just as the odd time . . . in her life . . . when clearly intended to be having pleasure . . . she was in fact . . . having none . . . not the slightest . . . in which case of course . . . that notion of punishment . . . for some sin or other . . . or for the lot . . . or no particular reason . . . for its own sake . . . thing she understood perfectly . . . that notion of punishment . . . which had first occurred to her . . . brought up as she had been to believe . . . with the other waifs . . . in a merciful . . . [*Brief laugh.*] . . . God . . . [*Good laugh.*] . . . first occurred to her . . . then dismissed . . . as foolish . . . was perhaps not so foolish . . . after all . . . so on . . . all that . . . vain reasonings . . . till another thought . . . oh long after . . . sudden flash . . . very foolish really but — . . . what? . . . the buzzing? . . . yes . . . all the time the buzzing . . . so-called . . . in the ears . . . though of course actually . . . not in the ears at all . . . in the skull . . . dull roar in the skull . . . and all the time this ray or beam . . . like moonbeam . . . but probably not . . . certainly not . . . always the same spot . . . now bright . . . now shrouded . . . but always the same spot . . . as no moon could . . . no . . . no moon . . . just all part of the same wish to . . . torment . . . though actually in point of fact . . . not in the least . . . not a twinge . . . so far . . . ha! . . . so far . . . this other thought then . . . oh long after . . . sudden flash . . . very foolish really but so like her . . . in a way . . . that she might do well to . . . groan . . . on and off . . . writhe she could not . . . as if in actual agony . . . but could not . . . could not bring herself . . . some flaw in her make-up . . . incapable of deceit . . . or the machine . . . more likely the machine . . . so disconnected . . . never got the message . . . or powerless to respond . . . like numbed . . . couldn't make the sound . . . not any sound . . . no sound of any kind . . . no screaming for help for example . . . should she feel so inclined . . . scream . . . [*Screams.*] . . . then listen . . . [*Silence.*] . . . scream again . . . [*Screams again.*] . . . then listen again . . . [*Silence.*] . . . no . . . spared that . . . all silent as the grave . . . no part — . . . what? . . . the buzzing? . . . yes . . . all silent but for the buzzing . . . so-called . . . no part of her moving . . . that she could feel . . . just the eyelids . . . presumably . . . on and off . . . shut out the light . . . reflex they call it . . . no feeling of any kind . . . but the lids . . . even best of times . . . who feels them? . . . opening . . . shutting . . . all that moisture . . . but the brain still . . . still sufficiently . . . oh very much so! . . . at this stage . . . in control . . . under control . . . to question even this . . . for on that April morning . . . so it reasoned . . . that April morning . . . she fixing with her eye . . . a distant bell . . . as she hastened towards it . . . fixing it with her eye . . . lest it elude her . . . had not all gone out . . . all that light . . . of itself . . . without any . . . any . . . on her part . . . so on . . . so on it reasoned . . . vain questionings . . . and all dead still . . . sweet silent as the grave . . . when suddenly . . . gradually . . . she realis— . . . what? . . . the buzzing? . . . yes . . . all dead still but for the buzzing . . . when suddenly she realised . . . words were — . . . what? . . . who? . . . no! . . . she! . . . [*Pause and movement 2.*] . . . realised . . . words were coming . . . imagine! . . . words were coming . . . a voice she did not recognise . . . at first . . . so long since it had sounded . . . then finally had to admit . . . could be none other . . . than her own . . . certain vowel sounds . . . she had never heard . . . elsewhere . . . so that people would stare . . . the rare occasions . . .

once or twice a year . . . always winter some strange reason . . . stare at her uncomprehending . . . and now this stream . . . steady stream . . . she who had never . . . on the contrary . . . practically speechless . . . all her days . . . how she survived! . . . even shopping . . . out shopping . . . busy shopping centre . . . supermart . . . just hand in the list . . . with the bag . . . old black shopping bag . . . then stand there waiting . . . any length of time . . . middle of the throng . . . motionless . . . staring into space . . . mouth half open as usual . . . till it was back in her hand . . . the bag back in her hand . . . then pay and go . . . not as much as good-bye . . . how she survived! . . . and now this stream . . . not catching the half of it . . . not the quarter . . . no idea . . . what she was saying . . . imagine! . . . no idea what she was saying! . . . till she began trying to . . . delude herself . . . it was not hers at all . . . not her voice at all . . . and no doubt would have . . . vital she should . . . was on the point . . . after long efforts . . . when suddenly she felt . . . gradually she felt . . . her lips moving . . . imagine! . . . her lips moving! . . . as of course till then she had not . . . and not alone the lips . . . the cheeks . . . the jaws . . . the whole face . . . all those — . . . what? . . . the tongue? . . . yes . . . the tongue in the mouth . . . all those contortions without which . . . no speech possible . . . and yet in the ordinary way . . . not felt at all . . . so intent one is . . . on what one is saying . . . the whole being . . . hanging on its words . . . so that not only she had . . . had she . . . not only had she . . . to give up . . . admit hers alone . . . her voice alone . . . but this other awful thought . . . oh long after . . . sudden flash . . . even more awful if possible . . . that feeling was coming back . . . imagine! . . . feeling coming back! . . . starting at the top . . . then working down . . . the whole machine . . . but no . . . spared that . . . the mouth alone . . . so far . . . ha! . . . so far . . . then thinking . . . oh long after . . . sudden flash . . . it can't go on . . . all this . . . all that . . . steady stream . . . straining to hear . . . make something of it . . . and her own thoughts . . . make something of them . . . all — . . . what? . . . the buzzing? . . . yes . . . all the time the buzzing . . . so-called . . . all that together . . . imagine! . . . whole body like gone . . . just the mouth . . . lips . . . cheeks . . . jaws . . . never — . . . what? . . . tongue? . . . yes . . . lips . . . cheeks . . . jaws . . . tongue . . . never still a second . . . mouth on fire . . . stream of words . . . in her ear . . . practically in her ear . . . not catching the half . . . not the quarter . . . no idea what she's saying . . . imagine! . . . no idea what she's saying! . . . and can't stop . . . no stopping it . . . she who but a moment before . . . but a moment! . . . could not make a sound . . . no sound of any kind . . . now can't stop . . . imagine! . . . can't stop the stream . . . and the whole brain begging . . . something begging in the brain . . . begging the mouth to stop . . . pause a moment . . . if only for a moment . . . and no response . . . as if it hadn't heard . . . or couldn't . . . couldn't pause a second . . . like maddened . . . all that together . . . straining to hear . . . piece it together . . . and the brain . . . raving away on its own . . . trying to make sense of it . . . or make it stop . . . or in the past . . . dragging up the past . . . flashes from all over . . . walks mostly . . . walking all her days . . . day after day . . . a few steps then stop . . . stare into space . . . then on . . . a few more . . . stop and stare again . . . so on . . . drifting around . . . day after day . . . or that time she cried . . . the one time she could remember . . .

since she was a baby . . . must have cried as a baby . . . perhaps not . . . not essential to life . . . just the birth cry to get her going . . . breathing . . . then no more till this . . . old hag already . . . sitting staring at her hand . . . where was it? . . . Croker's Acres . . . one evening on the way home . . . home! . . . a little mound in Croker's Acres . . . dusk . . . sitting staring at her hand . . . there in her lap . . . palm upward . . . suddenly saw it wet . . . the palm . . . tears presumably . . . hers presumably . . . no one else for miles . . . no sound . . . just the tears . . . sat and watched them dry . . . all over in a second . . . or grabbing at straw . . . the brain . . . flickering away on its own . . . quick grab and on . . . nothing there . . . on to the next . . . bad as the voice . . . worse . . . as little sense . . . all that together . . . can't — . . . what? . . . the buzzing? . . . yes . . . all the time the buzzing . . . dull roar like falls . . . and the beam . . . flickering on and off . . . starting to move around . . . like moonbeam but not . . . all part of the same . . . keep an eye on that too . . . corner of the eye . . . all that together . . . can't go on . . . God is love . . . she'll be purged . . . back in the field . . . morning sun . . . April . . . sink face down in the grass . . . nothing but the larks . . . so on . . . grabbing at the straw . . . straining to hear . . . the odd word . . . make some sense of it . . . whole body like gone . . . just the mouth . . . like maddened . . . and can't stop . . . no stopping it . . . something she — . . . something she had to — . . . what? . . . who? . . . no! . . . she! . . . [*Pause and movement 3.*] . . . something she had to — . . . what? . . . the buzzing? . . . yes . . . all the time the buzzing . . . dull roar . . . in the skull . . . and the beam . . . ferreting around . . . painless . . . so far . . . ha! . . . so far . . . then thinking . . . oh long after . . . sudden flash . . .

perhaps something she had to . . . had to . . . tell . . . could that be it? . . . something she had to . . . tell . . . tiny little thing . . . before its time . . . godforsaken hole . . . no love . . . spared that . . . speechless all her days . . . practically speechless . . . how she survived! . . . that time in court . . . what had she to say for herself . . . guilty or not guilty . . . stand up woman . . . speak up woman . . . stood there staring into space . . . mouth half open as usual . . . waiting to be led away . . . glad of the hand on her arm . . . now this . . . something she had to tell . . . could that be it? . . . something that would tell . . . how it was . . . how she — . . . what? . . . had been? . . . yes . . . something that would tell how it had been . . . how she had lived . . . lived on and on . . . guilty or not . . . on and on . . . to be sixty . . . something she — . . . what? . . . seventy? . . . good God! . . . on and on to be seventy . . . something she didn't know herself . . . wouldn't know if she heard . . . then forgiven . . . God is love . . . tender mercies . . . new every morning . . . back in the field . . . April morning . . . face in the grass . . . nothing but the larks . . . pick it up there . . . get on with it from there . . . another few — . . . what? . . . not that? . . . nothing to do with that? . . . nothing she could tell? . . . all right . . . nothing she could tell . . . try something else . . . think of something else . . . oh long after . . . sudden flash . . . not that either . . . all right . . . something else again . . . so on . . . hit on it in the end . . . think everything keep on long enough . . . then forgiven . . . back in the — . . . what? . . . not that either? . . . nothing to do with that either? . . . nothing she could think? . . . all right . . . nothing she could tell . . . nothing she could think . . . nothing she — . . .

what? . . . who? . . . no! . . . she! . . . [*Pause and movement 4.*] . . . tiny little thing . . . out before its time . . . godforsaken hole . . . no love . . . spared that . . . speechless all her days . . . practically speechless . . . even to herself . . . never out loud . . . but not completely . . . sometimes sudden urge . . . once or twice a year . . . always winter some strange reason . . . the long evenings . . . hours of darkness . . . sudden urge to . . . tell . . . then rush out stop the first she saw . . . nearest lavatory . . . start pouring it out . . . steady stream . . . mad stuff . . . half the vowels wrong . . . no one could follow . . . till she saw the stare she was getting . . . then die of shame . . . crawl back in . . . once or twice a year . . . always winter some strange reason . . . long hours of darkness . . . now this . . . this . . . quicker and quicker . . . the words . . . the brain . . . flickering away like mad . . . quick grab and on . . . nothing there . . . on somewhere else . . . try somewhere else . . . all the time something begging . . . something in her begging . . . begging it all to stop . . . unanswered . . . prayer unanswered . . . or unheard . . . too faint . . . so on . . . keep on . . . trying . . . not knowing what . . . what she was trying . . . what to try . . . whole body like gone . . . just the mouth . . . like maddened . . . so on . . . keep — . . . what? . . . the buzzing? . . . yes . . . all the time the buzzing . . . dull roar like falls . . . in the skull . . . and the beam . . . poking around . . . painless . . . so far . . . ha! . . . so far . . . all that . . . keep on . . . not knowing what . . . what she was — . . . what? . . . who? . . no! . . . she! . . . SHE! . . . [*Pause.*] . . . what she was trying . . . what to try . . . no matter . . . keep on . . . [*Curtain starts down.*] . . . hit on it in the end . . . then back . . . God is love . . .

tender mercies . . . new every morning . . . back in the field . . . April morning . . . face in the grass . . . nothing but the larks . . . pick it up —

[*Curtain fully down. House dark. Voice continues behind curtain, unintelligible, ten seconds, ceases as house lights up.*]

# Footfalls

Written in English. Begun in March 1975 and substantially completed by November of that year. First published by Grove Press, New York, in 1976. First performed at the Royal Court Theatre, London, on 20 May 1976, with Billie Whitelaw, directed by Samuel Beckett.

MAY (M), *dishevelled grey hair, worn grey wrap hiding feet, trailing.*

WOMAN'S VOICE (V) *from dark upstage.*

*Strip: downstage, parallel with front, length nine steps, width one metre, a little off centre audience right.*

```
      r  l  r  l  r  l  r  l  r  ←
L   ______________________________   R
      →  l  r  l  r  l  r  l  r  l
```

*Pacing: starting with right foot (r), from right (R) to left (L), with left foot (l) from L to R.*

*Turn: leftabout at L, rightabout at R.*

*Steps: clearly audible rhythmic tread.*

*Lighting: dim, strongest at floor level, less on body, least on head.*

*Voices: both low and slow throughout.*

*Curtain. Stage in darkness.*

*Faint single chime. Pause as echoes die.*

*Fade up to dim on strip. Rest in darkness.*

M *discovered pacing towards L. Turns at L, paces three more lengths, halts, facing front at R.*

*Pause.*

M: Mother. [*Pause. No louder.*] Mother.
[*Pause.*]

V: Yes, May.

M: Were you asleep?

V: Deep asleep. [*Pause.*] I heard you in my deep sleep. [*Pause.*] There is no sleep so deep I would not hear you there.

[*Pause.* M *resumes pacing. Four lengths. After first length, synchronous with steps.*] Seven eight nine wheel seven eight nine wheel. [*Free.*] Will you not try to snatch a little sleep?

[M *halts facing front at R. Pause.*]

M: Would you like me to inject you again?

V: Yes, but it is too soon.

[*Pause.*]

M: Would you like me to change your position again?

V: Yes, but it is too soon.

[*Pause.*]

M: Straighten your pillows? [*Pause.*] Change your drawsheet? [*Pause.*] Pass you the bedpan? [*Pause.*] The warming-pan? [*Pause.*] Dress your sores? [*Pause.*] Sponge you down? [*Pause.*] Moisten your poor lips? [*Pause.*] Pray with you? [*Pause.*] For you? [*Pause.*] Again.

[*Pause.*]

V: Yes, but it is too soon.

[*Pause.*]

M: What age am I now?

V: And I? [*Pause. No louder.*] And I?

M: Ninety.

V: So much?

M: Eighty-nine, ninety.

V: I had you late. [*Pause.*] In life. [*Pause.*] Forgive me again. [*Pause. No louder.*] Forgive me again.

[M *resumes pacing. After one length halts facing front at L. Pause.*]

M: What age am I now?

V: In your forties.

M: So little?

V: I'm afraid so. [*Pause.* M *resumes pacing. After first turn at R.*] May. [*Pause. No louder.*] May.

M: [*Pacing.*] Yes, Mother.

V: Will you never have done? [*Pause.*] Will you never have done . . . revolving it all?

M: [*Halting.*] It?

V: It all. [*Pause.*] In your poor mind. [*Pause.*] It all. [*Pause.*] It all.

[M *resumes pacing. Five seconds. Fade out on strip.*
*All in darkness. Steps cease.*
*Pause.*
*Chime a little fainter. Pause for echoes.*
*Fade up to a little less on strip. Rest in darkness.*
M *discovered facing front at R.*
*Pause.*]

V: I walk here now. [*Pause.*] Rather I come and stand. [*Pause.*] At nightfall. [*Pause.*] She fancies she is alone. [*Pause.*] See how still she stands, how stark, with her face to the wall. [*Pause.*] How outwardly unmoved. [*Pause.*] She has not been out since girlhood. [*Pause.*] Not out since girlhood. [*Pause.*] Where is she, it may be asked. [*Pause.*] Why, in the old home, the same where she — [*Pause.*] The same where she began. [*Pause.*] Where it began. [*Pause.*] It all began. [*Pause.*] But this, this, when did this begin? [*Pause.*] When other girls of her age were out at . . . lacrosse she was already here. [*Pause.*] At this. [*Pause.*] The floor here, now bare, once was — [M *begins pacing. Steps a little slower.*] But let us watch her move, in silence. [M *paces. Towards end of second length.*] Watch how feat she wheels. [M *turns, paces. Synchronous with steps third length.*] Seven, eight, nine, wheel. [M *turns at L, paces one more length, halts facing front at R.*] I say the floor here, now bare, this strip of floor, once was carpeted, a deep pile. Till one night, while still little more than a child, she called her mother and said, Mother, this is not enough. The mother: Not enough? May — the child's given name — May: Not enough. The mother: What do you mean, May, not enough, what can you possibly mean, May, not enough? May: I mean, Mother, that I must hear the feet, however faint they fall. The mother: The motion alone is not enough? May: No, Mother, the motion alone is not enough, I must hear the feet, however faint they fall. [*Pause.* M *resumes pacing. With pacing.*] Does she still sleep, it may be asked? Yes, some nights she does, in snatches, bows her poor head against the wall and snatches a little sleep. [*Pause.*] Still speak? Yes, some nights she does, when she fancies none can hear. [*Pause.*] Tells how it was. [*Pause.*] Tries to tell how it was. [*Pause.*] It all. [*Pause.*] It all.

[M *continues pacing. Five seconds. Fade out on strip.*
*All in darkness. Steps cease.*
*Pause.*
*Chime a little fainter still. Pause for echoes.*
*Fade up to a little less still on strip. Rest in darkness.*
M *discovered facing front at R.*
*Pause.*]

M: Sequel. [*Pause. Begins pacing. Steps a little slower still. After two lengths halts facing front at R. Pause.*] Sequel. A little later, when she was quite forgotten, she began to — [*Pause.*] A little later, when as though she had never been, it never been, she began to walk. [*Pause.*] At nightfall. [*Pause.*] Slip out at nightfall and into the little church by the north door, always locked at that hour, and walk, up and down, up and down. His poor arm. [*Pause.*] Some nights she would halt, as one frozen by some shudder of the mind, and stand stark still till she could move again. But many also were the nights when she paced without pause, up and down, up and down, before vanishing the way she came. [*Pause.*] No sound. [*Pause.*] None at least to be heard. [*Pause.*] The semblance. [*Pause. Resumes pacing. After two lengths halts facing front at R. Pause.*] The semblance. Faint, though by no means invisible, in a certain light. [*Pause.*] Given the right light. [*Pause.*] Grey rather than white, a pale shade of grey. [*Pause.*] Tattered. [*Pause.*] A tangle of tatters. [*Pause.*] Watch it pass — [*Pause.*] — watch her pass before the candelabrum, how its flames, their light . . . like moon through passing rack. [*Pause.*] Soon then after she was gone, as though never there, began to walk, up and down, up and down, that poor arm. [*Pause.*] At nightfall. [*Pause.*] That is to say, at certain seasons of the year, during Vespers. [*Pause.*] Necessarily. [*Pause. Resumes pacing. After one length halts facing front at L. Pause.*] Old Mrs Winter, whom the reader will remember, old Mrs Winter, one late autumn Sunday evening, on sitting down to supper with her daughter after worship, after a few half-hearted mouthfuls laid down her knife and fork and bowed her head. What is it, Mother, said the daughter, a most strange girl, though scarcely a girl any more . . . [*Brokenly.*] . . . dreadfully un— . . . [*Pause. Normal voice.*] What is it, Mother, are you not feeling yourself? [*Pause.*] Mrs W. did not at once reply. But finally, raising her head and fixing Amy — the daughter's given name, as the reader will remember — raising her head and fixing Amy full in the eye she said — [*Pause.*] — she murmured, fixing Amy full in the eye she murmured . . . Amy. Amy: Yes, Mother. Mrs W: did you observe anything . . . strange at Evensong? Amy: No, Mother, I did not. Mrs W: Perhaps it was just my fancy. Amy: Just what exactly, Mother, did you perhaps fancy it was? [*Pause.*] Just what exactly, Mother, did you perhaps fancy it was this . . . strange thing that you observed? [*Pause.*] Mrs W: You yourself observed nothing . . . strange? Amy: No, Mother, I myself did not, to put it mildly. Mrs W: What do you mean, Amy, to put it mildly, what can you possibly mean, Amy, to put it mildly? Amy: I mean, Mother, that to say I observed nothing . . . strange is indeed to put it mildly. For I observed nothing of any kind, strange or otherwise. I saw nothing, heard nothing, of any kind. I was not there. Mrs W: Not there? Amy: Not there. Mrs W: But I heard you respond. [*Pause.*] I heard you say Amen. [*Pause.*] How could you have responded if you were not there? [*Pause.*] How could you possibly have said Amen if, as you claim, you were not there? [*Pause.*] The love of God, and the fellowship of the Holy Ghost, be with us all, now, and for evermore. Amen. [*Pause.*] I heard you distinctly. [*Pause. Resumes pacing. After three steps halts without facing front. Long pause. Resumes pacing, halts facing front at R. Long pause.*] Amy. [*Pause. No louder.*] Amy. [*Pause.*] Yes, Mother. [*Pause.*] Will you never have done? [*Pause.*] Will you never have done . . . revolving it all? [*Pause.*] It? [*Pause.*] It all. [*Pause.*] In your poor mind. [*Pause.*] It all. [*Pause.*] It all.

[*Pause. Fade out on strip. All in darkness.*
*Pause.*
*Chime even a little fainter still. Pause for echoes.*
*Fade up to even a little less still on strip.*
*No trace of* MAY.
*Hold ten seconds.*
*Fade out.*]

CURTAIN

# Rockaby

Written in English between autumn 1979 and June 1980. First performed in Buffalo, NY, in 1981, played by Billie Whitelaw and directed by Alan Schneider. First published by Grove Press (1981), and in *Three Occasional Pieces* (Faber, 1982).

# Notes

*Light:*
Subdued on chair. Rest of stage dark.
Subdued spot on face constant throughout, unaffected by successive fades. Either wide enough to include narrow limits of rock or concentrated on face when still or at mid-rock. Then throughout speech face slightly swaying in and out of light.
Opening fade-up: first spot on face alone, long pause, then light on chair.
Final fade-out: first chair, long pause with spot on face alone, head slowly sinks, come to rest, fade out spot.

*W:*
Prematurely old. Unkempt grey hair. Huge eyes in white expressionless face. White hands holding ends of armrests.

*Eyes:*
Now closed, now open in unblinking gaze. About equal proportions section 1, increasingly closed 2 and 3, closed for good halfway through 4.

*Costume:*
Black lacy high-necked evening gown. Long sleeves. Jet sequins to glitter when rocking. Incongruous flimsy head-dress set askew with extravagant trimming to catch light when rocking.

*Attitude:*
Completely still till fade-out of chair. Then in light of spot head slowly inclined.

*Chair:*
Pale wood highly polished to gleam when rocking. Footrest. Vertical back. Rounded inward curving arms to suggest embrace.

*Rock:*
Slight. Slow. Controlled mechanically without assistance from W.

*Voice:*
Towards end of 4, say from 'saying to herself' on, gradually softer. Lines in italics spoken by W with V. A little softer each time, W's 'more' a little softer each time.

W: *Woman in chair.*
V: *Her recorded voice.*
*Fade up on* W *in rocking-chair facing front downstage slightly off centre audience left.*
*Long pause.*

W: More.
[*Pause. Rock and voice together.*]
V: till in the end
the day came
in the end came
close of a long day
when she said
to herself
whom else
time she stopped
*time she stopped*
going to and fro
all eyes
all sides
high and low
for another
another like herself
another creature like herself
a little like
going to and fro
all eyes
all sides
high and low
for another

till in the end
close of a long day
to herself
whom else
time she stopped
*time she stopped*
going to and fro
all eyes
all sides
high and low
for another
another living soul
going to and fro
all eyes like herself
all sides
high and low
for another
another like herself
a little like
going to and fro
till in the end
close of a long day
to herself
whom else
time she stopped
going to and fro
time she stopped
*time she stopped*

[*Together: echo of 'time she stopped', coming to rest of rock, faint fade of light.*
*Long pause.*]

W: More.

[*Pause. Rock and voice together.*]

V: so in the end
close of a long day
went back in

in the end went back in
saying to herself
whom else
time she stopped
*time she stopped*
going to and fro
time she went and sat
at her window
quiet at her window
facing other windows
so in the end
close of a long day
in the end went and sat
went back in and sat
at her window
let up the blind and sat
quiet at her window
only window
facing other windows
other only windows
all eyes
all sides
high and low
for another
at her window
another like herself
a little like
another living soul
one other living soul
at her window
gone in like herself
gone back in
in the end
close of a long day
saying to herself
whom else

time she stopped
*time she stopped*
going to and fro
time she went and sat
at her window
quiet at her window
only window
facing other windows
other only windows
all eyes
all sides
high and low
for another
another like herself
a little like
another living soul
one other living soul

[*Together: echo of 'living soul', coming to rest of rock, faint fade of light.*
*Long pause.*]

W: More.

[*Pause. Rock and voice together.*]

V: till in the end
the day came
in the end came
close of a long day
sitting at her window
quiet at her window
only window
facing other windows
other only windows
all blinds down
never one up
hers alone up
till the day came
in the end came

close of a long day
sitting at her window
quiet at her window
all eyes
all sides
high and low
for a blind up
one blind up
no more
never mind a face
behind the pane
famished eyes
like hers
to see
be seen
no
a blind up
like hers
a little like
one blind up no more
another creature there
somewhere there
behind the pane
another living soul
one other living soul
till the day came
in the end came
close of a long day
when she said
to herself
whom else
time she stopped
*time she stopped*
sitting at her window
quiet at her window
only window

facing other windows
other only windows
all eyes
all sides
high and low
time she stopped
*time she stopped*

[*Together: echo of 'time she stopped', coming to rest of rock, faint fade of light.*
*Long pause.*]

W: More.

[*Pause. Rock and voice together.*]

V: so in the end
close of a long day
went down
in the end went down
down the steep stair
let down the blind and down
right down
into the old rocker
mother rocker
where mother rocked
all the years
all in black
best black
sat and rocked
rocked
till her end came
in the end came
off her head they said
gone off her head
but harmless
no harm in her
dead one day
no
night

dead one night
in the rocker
in her best black
head fallen
and the rocker rocking
rocking away
so in the end
close of a long day
went down
in the end went down
down the steep stair
let down the blind and down
right down
into the old rocker
those arms at last
and rocked
rocked
with closed eyes
closing eyes
she so long all eyes
famished eyes
all sides
high and low
to and fro
at her window
to see
be seen
till in the end
close of a long day
to herself
whom else
time she stopped
let down the blind and stopped
time she went down
down the steep stair
time she went right down

was her own other
own other living soul
so in the end
close of a long day
went down
let down the blind and down
right down
into the old rocker
and rocked
rocked
saying to herself
no
done with that
the rocker
those arms at last
saying to the rocker
rock her off
stop her eyes
fuck life
stop her eyes
rock her off
rock her off

[*Together: echo of 'rock her off', coming to rest of rock, slow fade out.*]